THE LIBRARY OF INTERIOR DETAIL

VILLA

THE LIBRARY OF INTERIOR DETAIL

VILLA

Italian
Country Style

ELIZABETH HILLIARD

PHOTOGRAPHS BY JOHN MILLER

BULFINCH PRESS
LITTLE, BROWN AND COMPANY
BOSTON • NEW YORK • TORONTO • LONDON

First North American Edition

ISBN 0-8212-2171-X

Library of Congress Catalog Card Number 94-73028

Bulfinch Press is an imprint and trademark of
Little, Brown and Company (Inc.)
Published simultaneously in Canada by
Little, Brown & Company (Canada) Limited

PRINTED IN SINGAPORE

CONTENTS

INTRODUCTION
7

FLOORS, STAIRS AND CEILINGS
22

DOORS AND WINDOWS
30

PAINT
36

LIVING SPACES
46

FIREPLACES
54

KITCHENS
60

BEDROOMS AND BATHROOMS
70

ACKNOWLEDGEMENTS
80

A typical Tuscan jar with handles is a useful container for cooking implements. The flat 'spoon' with wooden prongs is used for stirring strands of pasta to loosen them in boiling water.

INTRODUCTION

Italian country style is a delicious mixture of traditions. Differences in cultural heritage and climate have given every region of this seductively beautiful country an identity and vernacular style of its own.

Just as building materials vary from one place to another, so methods of construction are adapted to suit the very different needs of local people. While a cedar-wood chalet in the Dolomites, for example, is built to keep out the snow, a white-painted stone *trullo* in Puglia – seven hundred miles south – is built to reflect the glare of the sun. The chalet undoubtedly has more in common with others across the border in Austria, the *trullo* with buildings in Greece, than either of them shares with houses the length of the peninsula in between. These contrasts mean not only that Italian country style is rich in local influences but also that it can be defined in a number of ways.

The vast majority of visitors to the Italian countryside flock to the central regions – Tuscany, principally, with an overflow into Umbria, the Marche and Lazio – and the domestic style most readily associated with Italy in the minds of foreigners is that of the stone-built central Italian villa or farmhouse. *Italian Country Style* reflects this tendency, devoting most of its pages to these regions, whose landscape, climate and way of life have produced, with minor variations, a distinct, and homogeneous style.

As a counterbalance, and as a demonstration of Italy's spectacular contrasts, a house in the far north of the country, at Cortina d'Ampezzo, is also included. Famous as a ski resort, Cortina, in Trentino-Alto Adige, is the capital of the Dolomites, often said to be the most beautiful mountains in the world. Here the climate is a more powerful influence than any other on the building style of the region. Typically, the older houses are constructed of a combination of wood and local stone, sometimes with superb lattice-work decoration on their upper storeys. Roofs are steeply pitched and overhang the walls by several feet to shed melting snow well away from the house. External wooden balconies running the length of south-facing walls make it possible, even in winter, to take a little exercise and enjoy the sun. In summer the carved balustrades of these balconies are festooned with baskets of flowers.

Internally, too, the walls, floors and ceilings of houses are constructed of wood to provide insulation. Antique furniture tends to be ornate compared with that of many other country districts, showing off the skill of local carpenters. As in any northern region, keeping warm in winter is a preoccupation; here the problem is often solved by a wood-burning stove. Some are magnificent – huge and highly decorative. Since they serve to heat the entire house, they are usually centrally sited in the kitchen.

One vital element that is common to country houses throughout Italy is the importance of the kitchen. For the *contadini*, or tenant farmers, of the past, the main event of the day, when all the family gathered together, was *pranzo*, or lunch. In the farmhouses of the central regions this was often eaten in a vast kitchen in which the only source of comfort was a wood fire burning on an enormous hearth. This leads to a central point about Italian country style: the family is the focus of everything. Italian households rich and poor revolve around the family; the arrangement and size of rooms, as well as their decoration, are geared to the family's essential social activities.

A detail of the fireplace illustrated on page 59, showing the putto's *head and wings.*

Outside walls in the lanes of towns and villages around Florence are often finished with decorative graffiti incised into the rough plaster. Made with a tool formed from nails hammered into a stick of wood, the patterns are wonderfully fresh because the artisan had only about twenty minutes before each panel of new plaster became too dry to work. This graffiti is unusual because it is indoors.

In the past, three or four generations lived together under one roof, and, though this is nowadays a rarity, far fewer Italians than Anglo-Saxons live alone. Even newly married couples often live with one or other set of parents for reasons of economy and convenience. The idea of privacy has until recently had little significance; even the word, *la privacy*, is new and imported.

If the family is the focus of life, the hearth is the symbol of family unity. In almost every traditional farmhouse, or *casa colonica*, the kitchen is dominated by a massive fireplace, watched over by the *nonna*, or grandmother, to ensure that the precious wood doesn't burn up too fast. In the past, heavy, blackened cauldrons, in which water was boiled and pasta was cooked for the midday meal, would have been suspended over the flames. Pasta is still made at home by many Italians, if only on special occasions, and every traditional kitchen has its pasta board and array of pasta-making utensils. A link with kitchens across the western world is provided by the familiar two-tier Moka coffee maker, which went into mass production after the Second World War. The Art Deco faceting on this delectable gadget makes it look like something between a Cubist's reinterpretation of the kettle and a lunar module. It is a design classic whose fresh, modern look belies its age. Without it no Italian kitchen would be complete.

Pre-war rural customs, especially where cookery is concerned, continue almost unchanged in many parts of Italy today. They are kept alive not just by *contadini* but also by middle-class country-house owning Italians who relish the chance to enjoy genuine, unpretentious country food.

The early decades of the twentieth century saw a considerable movement of Italians to North and South America, among other places, in search of work. Even today there are towns in such alien environments as the north of England where a restaurant or *trattoria* is almost entirely staffed by young men from the particular village in Italy whence the proprietor hails. In the 1950s and 1960s another exodus occurred as young people began to reject the hard work of life on the land in favour of more lucrative jobs in the cities. The farmhouses their families had inhabited for generations were gradually abandoned and fell into disrepair. As the market for such houses developed, so they began to come on the market, and in recent years Belgians, Germans, Dutch and umpteen others have joined the British in the rush for a rural idyll, with the result that every dilapidated tower and rustic haybarn from Liguria to Lazio is now being snapped up and converted.

The idea of doing up a place in the country is relatively new to the Italian professional classes. But Rome, Milan and other centres have become so chaotic in the past ten years that many people are now finding life intolerable without a bolt hole in the country to which they can retreat. Ilaria Miani is an example of an Italian who has caught the renovation bug. She and her family escape from Rome, where she has a business making reproduction antique furniture, to a farmhouse with stunning views over the Val d'Orcia, west of Montepulciano, the fourth house they have restored. 'The British, amongst other foreigners, really saw the potential in Tuscany and restored villas and farmhouses here', says Signora Miani. 'We owe them a great debt, though few Italians would like to admit it!'

Except in the most fashionable parts of Tuscany and Umbria, there is no shortage of desirable relics in agricultural areas. This is especially true of the south of Italy, or *Mezzogiorno*. But the trend is showing signs of slowing if not reversing as farming becomes more mechanized and modern housing more readily available. This new tendency does not, however, threaten the choice offered to someone looking for an old farmhouse, olive mill or granary to do up, as the type of home in demand from the local population is usually as new on the outside as it is easy-care on the inside.

Two magnificent pottery jugs of peasant design with wonderful depth and variation of colour in their glazes stand on a mid-nineteenth-century chest of drawers from the Veneto region of Italy.

Surrounded by a cluster of ancient outbuildings, the archetypal Italian farmhouse of everyone's dreams stands four-square on a Tuscan hilltop with a view over its own olive groves and vineyards that have scarcely changed since the fourteenth century. No wonder the idea of owning such a place has an irresistible appeal. The reality is that a country house or cow byre ripe for conversion will very likely have no mains water, road or sanitation. A building of any age and substance will, however, share some of the features common to the most beautiful examples of central Italian country style. It will be built of mellow local stone and roofed with lichen-covered *coppi* (the curved earthenware roof tiles to be found throughout the Mediterranean); its windows and doors, in the better buildings at least, will be framed in *travertine* or *pietra serena* (two types of dressed local stone), perhaps with faded shutters still intact; and it will form an integral part of the landscape to which it belongs.

A ceiling formed from pianelle, *thin bricks used for roofing (as here) or as a base for an upstairs floor, in which case terracotta tiles are placed on the bricks.*

Construction work is frequently overseen by a *geometra*, a man (almost invariably) who acts as site manager for an architect, combining some of the skills and knowledge of an architect and a surveyor with an invaluable understanding of the rules and regulations governing the restoration of old buildings. 'The rules seem to change every time we come out!' says one British owner of a renovated Tuscan farmhouse. 'The Italian authorities have woken up to conservation and are strict about your not altering the outside of old houses and even, sometimes, the inside. But we didn't find them officious or aggressive.'

The typical *casa colonica* is muscular, classically proportioned and uncompromising. Cosy it is not. Designed for coolness in the long, hot summers, its stone walls are often two feet (60cm) thick. The rooms are vast and unadorned, often the only ornament being a plastercast of the Madonna high on a wall. Since the *contadini* rarely owned the buildings in which they lived, had very little money and spent most of the hours of daylight out of doors, there was little incentive to embellish them. Furniture was minimal and often home made. When it broke it was either repaired with whatever came to hand or thrown away. As a result there is relatively little good antique country furniture in Italy compared with Britain, for example, where tenant farmers gained their independence much earlier, and, with it, a pride in home ownership. What there is is expensive. However, a good traditional piece, such as a panelled *cassapanca* (large chest) or *armadio* (wardrobe), originally the property of a country landowner, has the sort of integrity and simplicity that epitomize Italian country house style.

The most highly prized item of furniture in any Tuscan or Umbrian farmer's house was the matrimonial bed. This was an elaborate affair, traditionally made of wrought iron, the head decorated with curvilinear shapes framing a large, painted oval medallion depicting the Madonna or a local saint in a wreath of flowers. Today such beds are more likely to be found in the country homes of foreigners or city escapees, eager to adopt the trappings of a vanishing rural lifestyle, than in the houses of local people, who have long since discarded them in favour of modern mass-produced alternatives.

Another traditional piece of furniture now finding its way back to Tuscan and Umbrian farmhouses is the *madia*, a sort of chest on legs which was used in the past as a kneading trough for the making of bread. (Nowadays it more often serves as a drinks cabinet or cutlery store.) Almost all old country furniture that has survived the ravages of time is made of local chestnut, a weather-resistant and beautiful hardwood that is still used for the making of doors, window frames and furniture. Most houses would have had one or two cupboards built into the thickness of the walls of the kitchen to store food and crockery, a large table, a motley collection of wooden chairs, a stool or two by the fire and a few simple chests for clothes, linen and valuables. In the way of furniture they would have had little else.

Even as a weekend or holiday retreat, most city-dwellers would regard such simplicity as spartan, and have introduced the sort of creature comforts they are used to at home: easy chairs and settees, for instance, which are almost unknown in a *contadino* house. Nonetheless, the spacious, symmetrical rooms of Italian farmhouses lend themselves to being under furnished, and the simpler the furniture the more dramatic it looks against the granular, plastered walls.

Chairs are often arranged round the edge of the room rather than grouped in the middle, lending Italian country style a slightly formal air and a sense of organization. This has allowed it to assimilate elements of the clean-cut look which has made modern Italian fashion, furniture and household goods famous the world over: stylish lamps, for example, and the wonderfully elegant coffee pots designed by Alessi. In this way, new country house owners can have the best of both worlds, enjoying the textures of an ancient building and the products of local craftsmanship without sacrificing the convenience of labour-saving gadgetry or the beauty of modern Italian design.

A thrusting, city-dwelling couple, whose urban apartment is sleek and high-tech, will arrive at their country place and relax with a sigh of relief and a glass of red wine. Their *soggiorno*, or living room, like the rest of the house, is decorated to look unpretentious but smart in an understated way. Country style is relaxing because it is not intended to impress anyone; it is primarily for one's own comfort and enjoyment.

In most old farmhouses massive, hand-sawn chestnut beams support the ceilings, with narrower beams, or correntini, laid transversely to carry the weight of the floor tiles of the upper rooms. The most usual type of flooring is terracotta tiles – rectangular or,

On a fireplace mantelshelf stand two handsome pewter jars, inscribed with the initials of the owner and the date. These were used for transporting water or, more probably, wine on hunting trips.

less frequently, hexagonal in shape – with a scattering of rugs to soften and warm them in winter. Italy is the largest importer in the world, relative to its population, of Turkish and Persian carpets. In summer, terracotta floors are often left bare to show off the beauty of their surface, smoothed to a soft sheen by the passage of feet and undulating with age. In more modern houses and apartments, terrazzo tiling (marble chips laid in a mortar and highly polished) has largely taken over from terracotta as it is considered a great deal easier to keep clean.

An old chest with iron straps, handles and clasp stands sturdily on weathered terracotta tiles.

Most buildings in central and southern Italy have window shutters, frequently louvred, to filter the sun, and in the traditional *casa colonica* curtains are a rarity. Many foreign owners, however, particularly those from northern Europe, find bare window frames a little stark, and plain, unbleached calico or linen curtains can enhance the comfort of a room without detracting from its simplicity. For bed coverings and upholstery the subtle, earthy tones of vegetable-dyed fabrics are the perfect complement to the faded ochres and terracotta shades of the building itself.

Some of the grander and more elegant country houses have summer and winter drawing rooms, decorated in appropriate colours, the summer room pale and airy, the winter one furnished in darker, richer colours and with a fireplace as its focus. In addition there are smaller, more intimate rooms where the family gathers and friends are received.

Dilapidated farm buildings are ideal villa fodder in the sense that you can make pretty well what you want of a wreck. A significant distinguishing characteristic of proponents of country style, however, be they Italian, British or other, is their concern for a certain degree of authenticity. Ilaria Miani's team used construction stone which had tumbled from the crumbling building and was found in the undergrowth around the house, and interior walls were repaired using lime mortar. Although such skills as high quality stone masonry and the making of lime mortar have practically died out in many areas, it is still possible to find craftsmen willing and able to practise them, especially in central Italy where traditional materials and methods are in demand by the new wave of country house owners.

The Mianis found antique tiles for the upstairs and downstairs floors, and fittings large and small, from beams to doorknobs, to replace those stolen during the quarter century that the house was empty. Rooms have been simply painted, with wide bands of flat colour along the bottoms of walls and around doors. In many as yet unconverted houses the original tempera paint – strong pinks and blues for the most part – still clings to the peeling plaster of the walls, with a band of a darker colour below; this band is known as the *battiscopa* and served to disguise the marks left by the broom hitting the wall when sweeping the floor.

Despite a general desire for authenticity, there is one way in which old farmhouses throughout the country are almost invariably radically altered in the course of conversion. The ground floor originally served as a *stalla*, or cowshed; people lived upstairs. *Stalle* are now being turned into living rooms, complete with fireplaces, and kitchens

An elaborate closet for linen in a house in Cortina d'Ampezzo. The hand-carved panelling was made in 1941 from wood from the Arolla pine, Pinus cembra, *which grows in the area, and is finished with wax polish.*

are being moved from upstairs to downstairs. In the larger farmhouses, especially in the central regions, a striking feature of the *stalle* is often the magnificent brick-ribbed arches spanning the crypt-like interior space. Once converted, the ground floor provides a dramatic open-plan living area, sometimes using the wood from the *mangiatoio*, or manger – rubbed smooth by years of wear by feeding cattle – to make beautiful shelves or benches. Staircases, which were external and usually roofed, served only to provide access to living quarters upstairs.

At the Villa Cesia, near Rome, built between the eleventh and the fifteenth centuries, and restored in the twentieth by fashion designer Laura Biagiotti, the Milanese architect-designer Piero Pinto made the exciting discovery that there had been an internal staircase in former times, though the lower part had been filled in with earth. In other houses the architect has to juggle practical necessity with aesthetic and historical considerations to create a staircase and passages where there were none before.

In summer, outdoor space close to the house is used as an extra room, linked to the living rooms by french doors or, in modern conversions, by large expanses of sliding glass. One of the greatest delights of life here, as in all Mediterranean countries, is an *al fresco* lunch with family and friends under the dappled shade of a pergola dripping with grapes or wisteria.

The appeal of Italian country style is due, in no small part, to its application of traditional skills and materials to the demands of modern living. Walk into a house in rural Italy and you will feel a sense of ease in its well-proportioned rooms, and a timelessness that emanates from its classical simplicity and its relationship to the surrounding landscape.

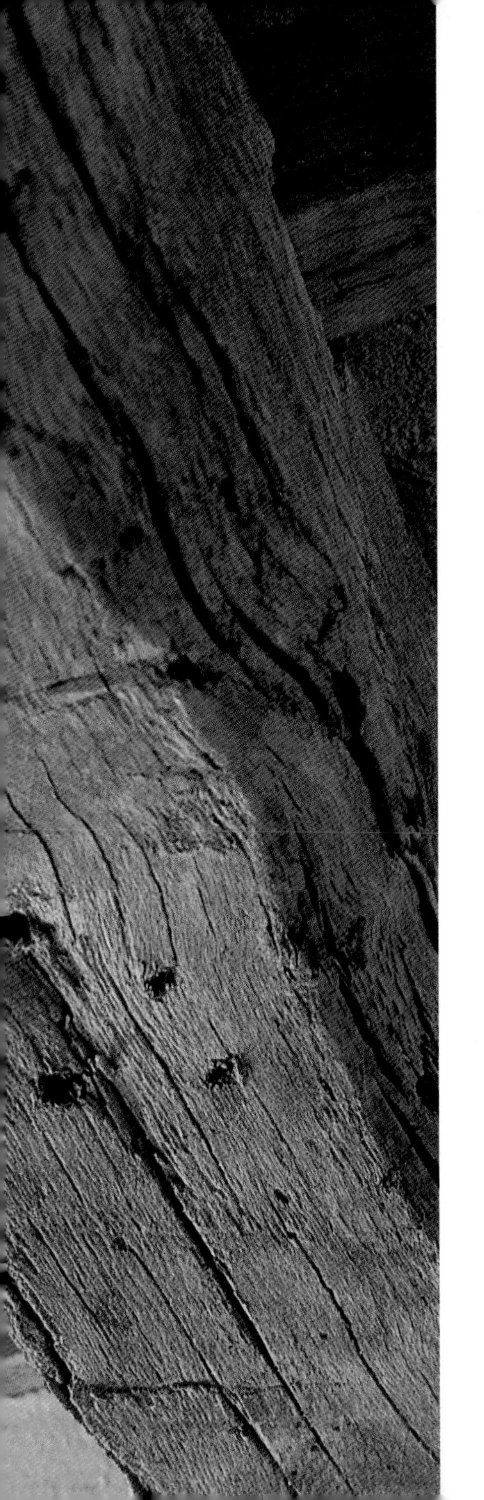

FLOORS, STAIRS & CEILINGS

THE FLOORS AND CEILINGS OF COUNTRY HOUSES IN ITALY ARE ROBUST AND UNPRETENTIOUS. A GRAND VILLA HAS TERRACOTTA TILES ON THE FLOOR, AND SO DOES A CONVERTED TUSCAN FARMHOUSE. SPLENDID WOODEN BEAMS SUPPORT CEILINGS AND ROOFS; SOLID STAIRCASES CARRY YOU FROM ONE FLOOR TO THE NEXT.

The ceiling of this downstairs room is made from large oak beams and smaller joists, on which are arranged thin bricks called pianelle. *The floor of the bedroom above is formed from terracotta tiles laid on these bricks.*

A stone staircase with painted iron balusters leads to the attics of a villa in the country near Florence, the summer home of an aristocratic family. The colour of the paint was popular at the end of the nineteenth century.

A newly formed indoor staircase in a renovated farmhouse. When the ground level of a farm building was inhabited by animals, the farmer and his family reached the upper floor by an outdoor staircase, today replaced by staircases such as this one.

The warm colour and worn appearance of these reclaimed terracotta tiles suggest centuries of use and have enduring appeal not only in the Italian countryside. The fashion for reclaimed terracotta means that such tiles are being rescued and exported for sale in countries across the world.

This type of Italian country kitchen, with a floor of reclaimed terracotta tiles, is not only practical and beautiful, but also inspires people all over the world to install 'farmhouse' kitchens of their own.

Above. *A ceiling contrasting with the one on pages 22–3, here constructed from sturdy beams, joists and planks instead of* pianelle, *thin bricks.*
Right. *The entire ceiling above the Tyrolean bed is whitewashed, beams and all.*

A vault constructed from terracotta tiles over a bathroom window. This room was formerly a pigsty, when the lower floor of the building was inhabited by animals and the upper floor by the farmer and his family.

DOORS & WINDOWS

EXTERNAL DOORS ARE ROBUST, INTERNAL DOORS DELICATE AND OFTEN ELEGANT. WINDOWS ARE DESIGNED TO PROTECT THE INTERIOR FROM THE BRILLIANT SUMMER SUNLIGHT, EITHER BY USE OF SMALL OPENINGS, WOODEN INTERIOR SHUTTERS OR, INTRIGUINGLY, BY CLEVER USE OF A PATTERN OF TERRACOTTA TILES SET ON THEIR ENDS AT ANGLES.

A heavy old door connecting one part of the terrace with another, in a wall roughly built of brick and stone. Originally painted a traditional strong green, it has faded in the sun to this shade of salvia, *or sage green.*

A magnificent, heavy wooden front door with iron bolts and hinges which would have been made by the local blacksmith. This example was found in a builders' yard, reclaimed and installed in a house which is part thirteenth century, part eighteenth century.

A bedroom door, again a simple affair made from planks painted with limewash and furnished with typically Tuscan ironmongery.

In 1929 this villa was redecorated and the door painted with pastoral scenes and an urn above. The artist was local and the decorations, which were standard in grand houses, were in a style popular from the end of the eighteenth century until well into the twentieth.

Terracotta tiles up-ended in a geometric pattern fill the outside of the kitchen window embrasure. Inside it is glazed, with the tiles creating shade from the sun without obscuring the view from the kitchen sink.

The restorers of this farmhouse have taken trouble to ensure that new windows are small, in keeping with the building's history. Peasant farmers did not want large window openings, making the house cold in winter and hot in summer. This casement opens inwards, and has glass in the panes and an interior shutter attached to the frame.

PAINT

PAINTED COLOUR IS USED IN MANY FLAMBOYANT WAYS IN ITALIAN COUNTRY HOUSES. IT PROVIDES ACCENTS ON WALLS AND AROUND DOORS AND WINDOWS; PAINTED DECORATION ENLIVENS THE FORMS OF ANTIQUE FURNITURE; AND THE LAYERS ARE SCRUBBED AWAY ON SIMPLE PEASANT FURNITURE TO REVEAL DECADES OF DIFFERENT COLOURS.

Appealingly distressed paintwork on an old cupboard reveals the many colours of paint applied over decades of use.

A shelf, formed from a niche in a wall, stores and displays wall paint used to decorate around doors, windows and this niche itself. The paints are traditional limewashes tinted with pigment. They have separated over time but the components mix again quickly if stirred, and these samples are kept for retouching and repairing worn areas.

Simple painted plank doors in the hall of a converted farmhouse. The hat hooks are typically Tuscan and would have been made by the village blacksmith. This interior is entirely decorated with limewash paint. White walls are enlivened by a variation on the traditional battiscopa, *a wide strip of colour along the base of the wall, intended to disguise marks made by the broom.*

Looking from one room to another, it is here possible to see at one glance several of the colours used to decorate this Tuscan farmhouse.

A piece of Indian fabric acts as a colourful tablecloth on a painted bedroom table. The floor is laid with terracotta tiles and covered with rugs, and the simple rustic chair is also painted in a contrasting red.

Like the kitchen cupboard on pages 36–7, this wardrobe has had the paint of decades scrubbed from it in such a way that the resulting effect is soft and mellow.

Above. *This marriage chest of 1873, painted with the date of the event, would have held sheets and other linen which the bride brought to her new home as part of her dowry.*

Left. *A handsome beam painted with the traditional lime-based paint which gradually flakes and peels as it ages.*

A painted wooden clock in a house in Cortina d'Ampezzo. The faux marble, flower-picture panels, decorative borders and a cut-out patterned base are typical of the Tyrol region of the Italian Alps, formerly part of Austria.

A magnificent example of a marriage wardrobe with the date of the wedding, 1830, painted on it. The delightful portraits on either side were found in a shop in Rome and show traditional Lombardy costumes of the later nineteenth century.

LIVING SPACES

INDOORS AND OUT, LIVING SPACES IN ITALIAN COUNTRY HOUSES ARE WELL-ORGANIZED IN A SIMPLE, RESTRAINED WAY WHICH BRINGS TOGETHER OLD AND NEW POSSESSIONS. A ROOM RARELY FEELS CROWDED WITH FURNITURE AND OBJECTS AND USUALLY HAS LITTLE OR NO CLUTTER. ELEGANCE AND COMFORT ARE ACHIEVED WITH APPARENT EFFORTLESSNESS.

A bench in the hall of the house in Tuscany. The English cotton fabric, from Designers Guild, is used one way on the seat cushion and back-to-front on the bolster.

An A-shaped wooden chest of drawers, typical of the Tyrolean furniture found in the Italian Alps.

Sets of chamois horns, hunters' trophies of the early nineteenth century, hang in a traditional geometric pattern in a house in Cortina d'Ampezzo in the Dolomite mountains in northern Italy.

A larger seation of the fresh and bold geometric pattern incised into rough plaster (see also page 10). This pattern is unusual in that it appears in a dining room whereas such graffiti was usually seen on external walls in the lanes of towns and villages around Florence.

A painted shutter at a window overlooking the drive of a villa in Tuscany. The shutters are eighteenth century and the tempera (egg based) paint is original. Decoration in this style was used all over the house and is common in other grand villas in the area.

Spring water gushes from the tap of a travertine marble sink on the terrace of a Tuscan farmhouse. Similar outdoor sinks were used by peasant farmers for drawing water, washing, and watering their livestock.

The terrace of a Tuscan farmhouse with the table set for a meal. This terrace has been newly created by the restorers of this farm building to provide a shady outdoor room, complete with vine-covered pergola. West-facing, it has breathtaking views over the Val d'Orcia.

FIREPLACES

THE FIREPLACE OR STOVE IS USUALLY THE ONLY FORM OF HEATING IN AN ITALIAN COUNTRY HOUSE AND IS OF VITAL IMPORTANCE. IN WINTER SUCH HOUSES ARE USUALLY TOO COLD FOR COMFORT AND THE INHABITANTS DECAMP TO THE CITY UNTIL SPRING. HOUSES IN THE MOUNTAINS, HOWEVER, ARE BUILT TO BE WARM IN WINTER.

A detail of the carved wooden fireplace on page 58, its pattern traditional and dateless.

A multi-tier wood-burning stove of the type which was once used for heating rooms in superior farmhouses in the Tuscan countryside. An elaborate example in a grand villa might have six tiers, be highly ornate and might even be glazed. The fire irons are for bellezza; *in fact all you need to operate the stove is a shovel.*

A wide open downhearth in the sitting room of a Tuscan house gives ample heat on cool days and evenings.

One of the magnificent stone buttresses supporting the stone mantel shelf over the fireplace left.

A warming scene in winter. The fire surround was hand carved in 1941, when this house in Cortina d'Ampezzo was fitted out, but the design is traditional to this area and is dateless. The gilded clock is early nineteenth century and was brought from Turin.

The head and wings of a putto *or cherub which looks out from a seventeenth-century limestone and marble fireplace, bought and installed in 1929. The fire is never lit in winter because the house is so cold that the family abandons it and moves to Florence.*

KITCHENS

ITALIAN FAMILY LIFE REVOLVES AROUND MEALTIMES AND THE KITCHEN, WHICH IS USUALLY A WELCOMING ROOM WITH A LARGE TABLE. POTS AND PANS ARE ON DISPLAY ON WALLS OR HANGING FROM CEILINGS; FAMILIAR OLD FURNITURE ADDS TO THE FRIENDLINESS OF THE ROOM, AND FRESH VEGETABLES WAITING FOR PREPARATION LEND SPASHES OF BRIGHT COLOUR.

A kitchen work surface formed from the ubiquitous terracotta tiles, with luscious vegetables and herbs waiting to be prepared for cooking.

Before this farmhouse was renovated the family kitchen was a stable. Animals lived on the ground floor of such buildings and the farmer and his wife above. Traditional baskets and pans hang from the ceiling.

The owner of this kitchen found the hand-hewn stone sink in the grounds when restoring her house near Florence. The kitchen, which is predictably used for eating as well as preparing and cooking food, is decorated with hand-made tiles and plates from Amalfi, south of Naples, famous for its pottery.

A massive pine laundry cupboard in a guardaroba, *an ante room to the kitchen, in a large villa in Tuscany.*

Ripe watermelon and apples, bought in the local market, rest in nineteenth-century wooden peasant-made bowls on top of a pine kitchen cupboard.

Una madia, *literally a bread bin, but actually more of a cupboard. The front and top fold back, to provide access to the space for storing flour as well as bread.*

A traditional ham stand hanging from a beam in the kitchen. When you lay it on the counter, the feet stick up and hold the prosciutto firm for carving. This stand is modern but the same design has been in use for centuries in Italian kitchens.

Built into the walls of an eighteenth-century Tuscan house, this bread oven was operated by building a fire and pushing it to one side once it had burnt down and heated the interior. Loaves were then inserted and later removed when cooked with the flat iron shovel.

A sink made of pietra serena *in the pantry, in the late eighteenth-century part of a villa. The tiles are something of a joke in the aristocratic family whose summer home this is, because they show their coat of arms (given in 1701) back to front.*

BEDROOMS & BATHROOMS

IN AN ITALIAN COUNTRY HOUSE WHERE THE BEAMED BEDROOM CEILING IS PAINTED WITH TRADITIONAL WHITEWASH, YOU ARE GRATEFUL FOR A BED WHICH GIVES YOU A ROOF OVER YOUR HEAD TO PROTECT YOU FROM FALLING FLAKES OF PAINT. BATHROOMS IN CONVERTED FARM-HOUSES ARE ALWAYS MODERN.

A bathroom floor covered in the early years of the twentieth century with tiles decorated in a style popular from the end of the previous century. The tiles were probably made at Impruneta, near Florence, where ceramics are still made today.

A modern interpretation of a traditional Tyrolean bed, in a house in central Italy. The height of the mattress means you can see out of the window when lying on the bed, and there is room underneath for storing things. The top of the bed protects you from flakes of paint falling from the whitewashed ceiling.

A pair of beds from Laboratorio Ilaria Miani in the Mianis' Tuscan home. Inspired by the dignified simplicity of Shaker furniture, the beds are painted and draped with Indian muslin, again to protect the sleeper from falling fragments of limewash.

A fresh and uncluttered bedroom furnished with painted pieces such as the wardrobe, and folding furniture like the butler's tray, a modern reinterpretation of a classic piece of furniture.

This magnificent polished, carved and gilded bedhead was made near Florence for Senator Ferrante Capponi, a Florentine nobleman who died in 1689. It is still in the Capponi family villa.

Alongside this closet is a small painting of a detail of northern European costume, the back of a woman's head showing her elaborate lace or crocheted cap.

A painted marriage wardrobe, brought by the bride as part of her dowry, in a bedroom in northern Italy.

Bathrooms in converted farm buildings are always, inevitably, modern. Here the bath has been surrounded with old terracotta tiles. The photograph frame is modern, based on gilded flower designs found on antique Japanese kimono boxes.

The owner of this Tuscan house has a taste for round basins. These are set into polished peperino, below mirrors with frames made at the Laboratorio Ilaria Miani in Rome. The plumbing beneath is disguised with simple painted paling.

ACKNOWLEDGEMENTS

DEDICATION

To the memory of my friend, the late Lollj Bertin

Elizabeth Hilliard would like to thank the many people whose kindness and enthusiasm have helped her with this book, but she is especially grateful to the following: June Bellamy; Felicity Bryan and Michele Topham; Paul Burcher; Contessa Capponi; Katrin Cargill; Wendy Dallas; Karen Hill; Alan James; Rachel King; Laurence Krzyzanek; Ilaria Miani, whose designs can be found at the Laboratorio Ilaria Miani, via Orti d'Alibert 13/a, 00165 Rome (tel/fax 6861366), Helen Selka Farmiloe; William Selka; Emanuela Stucchi Prinetti; Mrs David Waterhouse; Rebecca Willis.

Above all, she thanks John Miller whose beautiful photographs make this book what it is.